AF585696

Exploring The Depths of Emotional Well-Being

"A Journey of Self-Discovery"

WEALTH SPACE

All right reserved. No part of this publication may be reproduced, distributed, or transmitted in any form or by any means, including photocopying, recording, or other electronic or mechanical methods, without the prior written permission of the publisher, except in the case of brief quotations embodied in critical reviews and certain other noncommercial uses permitted by copyrighted law.

Copyright © Wealth Space

INTRODUCTION

Emotional well-being is an integral aspect of overall health and happiness. It refers to the ability to regulate and manage one's emotions healthily and adaptively, as well as to experience a range of positive emotions and a sense of overall satisfaction with life. Exploring the depths of emotional well-being involves embarking on a journey of self-discovery, in which individuals can learn more about themselves, their emotional experiences, and the factors that impact their emotional well-being.

There are many different approaches to exploring emotional well-being. Some people may choose to work with a mental health professional, such as a therapist or counselor, to learn more about their emotions and how to manage them. Others may prefer to engage in self-exploration through activities such as journaling, mindfulness practices, or creative expression.

One important aspect of exploring emotional well-being is becoming more aware of one's own emotions. This involves paying attention to the emotions that arise in daily life, as well as the thoughts, behaviors, and physical sensations that are associated with those emotions. It can also involve reflecting on past experiences and the emotions that were present in those situations. By becoming more aware of one's emotions, individuals can better understand the triggers that lead to certain emotional experiences and develop strategies for healthily managing those emotions.

Another important aspect of exploring emotional well-being is learning how to effectively communicate and express emotions. This involves finding healthy ways to express and cope with difficult emotions, such as anger, sadness, or anxiety, as well as finding ways to communicate and share positive emotions with others. It may also involve learning how to set boundaries and assert oneself in relationships, to ensure that one's emotional needs are met.

In addition to these personal skills, there are also external factors that can impact emotional well-being. These can include things like relationships, work, financial circumstances, physical health, and social support. By exploring these factors and learning how to manage them healthily, individuals can improve their emotional well-being.

There are many tools and resources available to support individuals in their journey of self-discovery and emotional well-being. These can include therapy or counseling, self-help books and articles, support groups, and online resources. It is important to find the approach that works best for each individual, as everyone has unique needs and preferences when it comes to exploring their emotional well-being.

However, exploring the depths of emotional well-being is an important and ongoing process that involves becoming more aware of one's own emotions, developing effective communication and expression skills, and managing external factors that can impact emotional well-being. By embarking on this journey of self-discovery, individuals can learn more about themselves and develop the skills and strategies needed to cultivate greater emotional well-being and overall health and happiness.

It is important to remember that emotional well-being is an ongoing process and that there is no “quick fix” to improving emotional health. Exploring the depths of emotional well-being requires an ongoing commitment to self-discovery and learning, as well as a willingness to experiment with different approaches and tools. By taking the time to explore emotional well-being, individuals can gain a deeper understanding of themselves and how they can cultivate greater emotional health and well-being

CHAPTER 1:

What is emotional well-being and why is it important?

Emotional well-being is a state of being that involves the ability to experience and express a range of emotions, as well as the capacity to cope with and manage stress. It is an important aspect of overall health and well-being, as it can significantly impact our daily lives and long-term success.

Emotional well-being is closely related to mental health, which is defined as the state of being mentally and emotionally stable and functioning effectively. Mental health disorders, such as anxiety and depression, can have a significant impact on a person's emotional well-being. However, even those without a diagnosable mental health disorder can experience poor emotional well-being if they struggle to manage their emotions or cope with stress.

Several factors can contribute to emotional well-being, including social support, a sense of purpose and meaning in life, and a sense of control over one's circumstances. Physical health and self-care practices, such as exercising and getting enough sleep, can also play a role in emotional well-being.

One of the key components of emotional well-being is the ability to experience and express a range of emotions. This includes both positive emotions, such as happiness, love, and gratitude, as well as negative emotions, such as sadness, anger, and fear. It is important to recognize and accept all emotions, rather than trying to suppress or ignore them. This allows us to better understand and navigate our experiences and can help us build resilience in the face of challenges.

In addition to experiencing and expressing emotions, it is also important to have the skills and strategies to cope with and manage stress. This can include finding healthy ways to relax and unwind, setting boundaries and managing time effectively, and seeking support from friends, family, or a mental health professional when needed.

Emotional well-being is important for several reasons. It can impact our relationships with others, as well as our ability to succeed in work and other areas of life. When we are emotionally well, we are better able to form and maintain meaningful connections with others, and we are more resilient in the face of challenges. In contrast, poor emotional well-being can lead to difficulty forming and maintaining relationships, as well as an increased risk of mental health disorders.

Emotional well-being is also important for physical health. Chronic stress and negative emotions can hurt the body, increasing the risk of physical health problems such as heart disease, high blood pressure, and weakened immune function. In contrast, positive emotions and good emotional well-being can have a protective effect on physical health.

There are several ways to promote and maintain emotional well-being. Some of the strategies include:

- Engaging in self-care practices, such as exercising, getting enough sleep, and eating a healthy diet
- Finding healthy ways to relax and unwind, such as through meditation, yoga, or spending time in nature
- Setting boundaries and managing time effectively to reduce stress
- Seeking support from friends, family, or a mental health professional when needed
- Engaging in activities that bring meaning and purpose to life, such as volunteering or pursuing hobbies
- Practicing gratitude and positive thinking

Emotional well-being is a crucial aspect of overall health and well-being. It involves the ability to experience and express a range of emotions, as well as the capacity to cope with and manage stress. By prioritizing self-care and seeking support when needed, we can work to promote and maintain good emotional well-being. In doing so, we can improve our relationships, our ability to succeed in work and other areas of life, and our physical health.

The Role of Self-Discovery in Emotional Well-Being

Self-discovery is the process of learning about one's thoughts, feelings, values, beliefs, and behaviors. It is a journey of self-exploration that can help individuals gain a better understanding of themselves and their place in the world. This process of self-discovery can be a powerful tool for promoting emotional well-being, as it allows individuals to gain insight into their own emotions and how they can effectively manage them.

One way that self-discovery can promote emotional well-being is by helping individuals to identify and understand their emotional triggers. Many people have certain situations or events that consistently elicit strong emotional responses from them. By engaging in self-discovery, individuals can learn to recognize these triggers and identify the underlying emotions that are driving their reactions. This self-awareness can help individuals to better manage their emotions and avoid becoming overwhelmed by them.

Another benefit of self-discovery is that it can help individuals to develop emotional intelligence, or the ability to recognize and understand emotions in themselves and others. This is important because emotional intelligence is closely linked to overall well-being and mental health. By learning more about their own emotions, individuals can become more attuned to the emotional needs of others and be better able to navigate social situations and relationships.

Self-discovery can also help individuals to identify and address any emotional challenges or issues they may be facing. By examining their thoughts, feelings, and behaviors, individuals may discover patterns or behaviors that are contributing to negative emotional states. For example, an individual may realize that they tend to ruminate on negative thoughts, which can lead to feelings of sadness or anxiety. By becoming aware of these patterns, individuals can work to change them and adopt more positive coping strategies.

Self-discovery can also be a valuable tool for promoting personal growth and development. By learning more about themselves, individuals can identify their strengths and weaknesses and set goals for personal growth and self-improvement. This process can help individuals to feel more fulfilled and satisfied with their lives, which can contribute to overall emotional well-being.

There are many different ways that individuals can engage in self-discovery, including through therapy, journaling, mindfulness practices, and self-reflection. Each person will have a unique path to self-discovery, and individuals need to find the methods that work best for them. It is also important to remember that self-discovery is a lifelong process, and individuals should be open to ongoing self-exploration and learning.

Self-discovery can be a challenging and sometimes uncomfortable process, as it may involve facing difficult emotions and personal challenges. However, it can also be a deeply rewarding experience that can lead to greater self-awareness, emotional intelligence, and overall well-being. By committing to the process of self-discovery, individuals can learn to understand and manage their emotions healthily and effectively, leading to a more fulfilling and satisfying life.

The role of self-discovery in emotional well-being is an important one, as it helps individuals to gain insight into their own emotions, understand the triggers of their emotional responses, develop emotional intelligence, identify and address any emotional challenges they may be facing, and promote personal growth and development. Self-discovery can be a difficult but rewarding journey, and individuals need to be open to learning and exploring their inner selves. By engaging in this process, individuals can gain a better understanding of themselves and their emotions and promote greater emotional well-being.

Tips and Strategies to the role of self-recovery in emotional well-being.

1. **Develop Self-awareness:** Self-awareness is an important part of self-discovery and emotional well-being. It involves understanding your own emotions, thoughts, beliefs, and behaviors and how they affect your life. Developing self-awareness can help you recognize and understand your emotional triggers, identify patterns in your behavior, and make changes to improve your emotional well-being.

2. **Use Self-reflection:** Self-reflection is a powerful tool for self-discovery and emotional well-being. It involves taking time to think about your life, your values, and your beliefs. You can use self-reflection to gain a deeper understanding of yourself and your emotions and to identify areas of your life that need to be addressed or improved.

3. **Practice Mindfulness:** Mindfulness is a powerful practice for self-discovery and emotional well-being. It involves being present at the moment and allowing yourself to observe and be aware of your thoughts and feelings without judgment. Mindfulness can help you become more aware of your emotional triggers, better understand your emotions and reactions, and learn how to manage them healthily.

4. Seek Professional help: If you feel like you need help with self-discovery and emotional well-being, then it may be beneficial to seek professional help. Talking to a therapist or counselor can be a great way to gain insight into your emotions, develop coping strategies, and make positive changes in your life.

5. Talk to people: Talking to friends, family, or other people who understand your experiences and feelings can be a great way to gain perspective and promote emotional well-being. Talking to someone supportive and non-judgmental can help you feel heard and understood. You can also use these conversations to gain insight into yourself and your emotional landscape.

Self-discovery can be a powerful tool for promoting emotional well-being and overall mental health. By engaging in self-awareness, self-reflection, mindfulness, and seeking professional help, individuals can gain a better understanding of themselves and their emotions and learn how to manage them healthily and effectively. This process of self-discovery can lead to greater emotional intelligence, personal growth and development, and overall satisfaction with life.

6. Explore your passions: Exploring your passions and interests can be a great way to gain insight into yourself and your emotions. By engaging in activities and hobbies that you enjoy, you can gain a better understanding of what makes you feel fulfilled and satisfied. This can help you identify areas of your life that need to be addressed or changed to promote emotional well-being.

7. Take care of your physical health: Taking care of your physical health can have a positive impact on your emotional well-being. Eating a healthy diet, getting enough sleep, and exercising regularly can help you feel better emotionally and mentally.

8. Connect with Nature: Connecting with nature can be a great way to relax, gain perspective, and practice mindfulness. Spending time in nature can help you feel more grounded and connected to the world around you.

9. Journal: Writing down your thoughts and feelings can be a great way to gain insight into yourself and your emotions. Writing can help you identify patterns in your behavior and understand your emotional triggers.

10. Practice gratitude: Practicing gratitude can help you focus on the positive aspects of your life and create a more positive outlook. Focusing on what you are grateful for can help you feel more connected to the world and more satisfied with your life.

11. Set boundaries: Setting boundaries is important for self-care and emotional well-being. Knowing when to say no and how to protect yourself from unhealthy situations can help you feel more in control of your life and better manage your emotions.

12. Seek out meaningful relationships: Connecting with people who understand and support you can be a great way to promote emotional well-being. Having meaningful relationships with people you trust and care about can help you feel heard and understood and can provide a sense of belonging.

13. Spend time alone: Spending time alone can be beneficial for self-reflection, self-care, and emotional well-being. Taking time to be alone can help you reconnect with yourself and your emotions and better understand what you need to promote emotional well-being.

14. Learn to be flexible: Being flexible and open to change can help you better manage your emotions and adapt to life's challenges. Learning to accept change and go with the flow can help you feel more in control of your life and better handle stressful situations.

15. Take time to relax: Taking time to relax and engage in activities that you find calming and enjoyable can help you manage your emotions and reduce stress.

16. Find a support system: Having a strong support system of family, friends, and professionals can be beneficial for emotional well-being. Knowing that you have people who understand and support you can help you feel less alone and more connected to the world.

17. Make time for fun: Making time for activities that bring you joy and pleasure can help you feel more connected to the world and more satisfied with your life.

18. Learn to forgive: Forgiveness is an important part of emotional well-being. Learning to forgive yourself and others can help you move past negative emotions and promote greater peace of mind.

19. Seek help when needed: It is important to seek help when needed. Talking to a therapist, counselor, or another mental health professional can be beneficial for self-discovery and emotional well-being.

20. Be kind to yourself: Being kind to yourself is an important part of self-care and emotional well-being. Learning to treat yourself with kindness and compassion can help you develop a greater sense of self-worth and promote a more positive outlook.

CHAPTER II.

Understanding Your Emotions

Emotions are an integral part of our lives, shaping how we think, feel, and behave. They can range from positive emotions such as happiness and gratitude to negative emotions like anger and fear. Understanding our emotions is important because it allows us to better understand ourselves, our motivations, and our actions. It can also help us to better understand and connect with others, as well as manage and regulate our emotions in healthy ways.

So, how can we go about understanding our emotions? One helpful way is to practice mindfulness, which involves paying attention to our thoughts and feelings in a non-judgmental way. This can help us to become more aware of our emotions as they arise, rather than being caught off guard by them or reacting automatically.

Another way to understand our emotions is to practice self-reflection. This involves taking time to think about our emotions and what might have caused them. For example, if we feel anxious, we can ask ourselves what might be causing that anxiety and if there is anything we can do to address it.

It can also be helpful to talk about our emotions with others, such as a friend, family member, or therapist. This can help us to better understand and process our emotions, as well as receive support and perspective from others.

Emotions can also be influenced by our thoughts and beliefs. For example, if we have negative thoughts about ourselves or a situation, we may feel sad or anxious. On the other hand, if we have positive thoughts and beliefs, we may feel happier and more confident. It can be helpful to pay attention to our thoughts and try to reframe them more positively when necessary.

It's also important to recognize that emotions are not always rational or logical. They can be influenced by a variety of factors, including past experiences, cultural norms, and even hormones. This is why it's important to try to understand and acknowledge our emotions, rather than judging or dismissing them.

Another way to better understand our emotions is to learn about different emotional states and what they might mean. For example, fear is a natural emotion that is often triggered by perceived threats or dangers. Anger is often a response to feeling threatened or wronged in some way. Sadness is often a natural response to loss or disappointment. Joy is a positive emotion that can be triggered by happy events or experiences.

It's also important to recognize that emotions can be complex and layered, and it's not uncommon to feel multiple emotions at the same time. For example, we may feel both anxious and excited about a job interview, or both sad and relieved when a relationship ends.

It's also worth noting that there is no one "right" way to feel about any given situation. Different people may have different emotional responses to the same event, and that's okay. It's important to respect and validate others' emotions, even if they differ from our own.

In summary, understanding our emotions is an important part of self-awareness and self-regulation. It involves paying attention to our thoughts, feelings, and behaviors, as well as practicing mindfulness, self-reflection, and seeking support from others when needed. It's also important to recognize that emotions are complex and can be influenced by a variety of factors. By better understanding our emotions, we can learn to manage and regulate them in healthy ways, which can help us to lead more fulfilling and meaningful lives.

The good news is that understanding our emotions is something that we can all work on. With practice and dedication, we can become more aware of our emotions, better understand them, and learn how to manage them in healthy ways.

The different types of emotions and how to identify them

Emotions are one of the most complex and fascinating aspects of the human experience. They can range from intense joy and excitement to deep sadness and fear. While each emotion is unique and individual, it can be broadly categorized into different types.

Knowing and understanding the different types of emotions can help us better identify and express our feelings, as well as empathize with others.

The four main types of emotions are:

1. **Positive Emotions** – These emotions include joy, happiness, excitement, love, gratitude, and contentment. They are generally associated with pleasant experiences and can help us feel connected to others.

2. **Negative Emotions** – These emotions include anger, fear, sadness, anxiety, shame, and guilt. They can be difficult to experience but can be important for helping us recognize when something is wrong or unsafe.

3. **Social Emotions** – These emotions include admiration, admiration, embarrassment, envy, jealousy, and pride. They can help us navigate social situations and foster relationships with others.

4. **Cognitive Emotions** – These emotions include surprise, interest, confusion, and boredom. They are related to thinking and can help us better understand the world around us.

IDENTIFYING EMOTIONS

The first step to understanding and expressing emotions is to be able to identify them. This can be tricky, as emotions can be complex and manifest in different ways. However, there are a few strategies that can help us better recognize and name our emotions.

1. Notice Your Physical Sensations – Our bodies often provide us with clues about how we are feeling. Paying attention to physical sensations such as rapid breathing, a pounding heart, or a tense stomach can help us better identify our emotions.

2. Pay Attention to Your Thoughts – Our thoughts can also provide us with clues about our emotions. Notice if you are having thoughts that are negative or positive, and see if you can identify the emotion behind them.

3. Ask Yourself Questions – Asking yourself questions can help you better understand your emotions. For example, if you are feeling angry, you could ask yourself "What is making me angry?" or "What do I need right now?"

4. Talk to A Friend – Talking to a trusted friend or family member can also be a helpful way to identify and understand your emotions. Explaining how you are feeling to someone else can help you gain clarity on your experience.

EXPRESSING EMOTIONS

Once we have identified our emotions, the next step is learning how to express them in healthy ways. This can be a difficult process, especially if we have been taught to repress our feelings. However, expressing our emotions can be an important part of self-care and is key to building strong relationships.

1. Talk About Your Feelings – Talking to someone about your emotions can be a great way to release pent-up energy. Choose someone supportive and understanding, and explain how you are feeling in a calm and non-blaming way.

2. Write It Down – Writing can be a great way to express our emotions. Get out a pen and paper and let your feelings flow. You can also write a letter to yourself or someone else, expressing how you feel.

3. Express Yourself Creatively – Creative activities such as drawing, painting, or playing music can also be great ways to express your emotions. Let your inner artist out and let your emotions guide your work.

4. Move Your Body – Moving your body is a great way to release emotional energy. Take a walk, do some yoga or dance around your house. Allow yourself to let go and express yourself through movement.

MANAGING EMOTIONS

Learning how to manage our emotions is an important part of self-care. Managing our emotions can help us prevent unnecessary stress and worry, as well as make healthier decisions.

1. Take a Break – Stepping away from a difficult situation can be a helpful way to manage our emotions. Take a few deep breaths, go for a walk, or take a break from the situation. This can help us gain perspective and come back with a clearer head.

2. Practice Self-Care – Practicing self-care activities can help us better manage our emotions. Take a warm bath, listen to music, or do something that lifts your spirits.

3. Connect with Nature – Connecting with nature can help us feel calmer and more grounded. Taking a walk in a park or going for a swim can help us release stress and emotions.

4. Talk to a Professional – Seeing a therapist or counselor can be a great way to learn how to better manage your emotions. They can provide you with the tools and support to better understand and express your feelings.

The Importance of learning to recognize and label your emotions

Learning to recognize and label your emotions is an important skill that can benefit you in many areas of your life. It can help you understand yourself better, communicate more effectively with others, and make better decisions. It can also help you cope with stress and lead a more fulfilling life.

One of the key benefits of learning to recognize and label your emotions is that it can help you better understand yourself and your motivations. When you can identify and name your emotions, it becomes easier to reflect on what is causing them and why you are experiencing them. This self-awareness can help you make more informed decisions about your actions and behaviors.

For example, if you are feeling angry, you may be more likely to lash out or make impulsive decisions. By recognizing and labeling this emotion, you can take a step back and consider whether this is the best course of action. You may choose to take a break, find a healthy outlet for your anger, or seek support from a trusted friend or family member.

Another benefit of learning to recognize and label your emotions is that it can help you communicate more effectively with others. When you can accurately express how you are feeling, it can be easier for others to understand you and respond in a supportive way. This can be especially important in relationships, where effective communication is key to building trust and resolving conflicts.

For example, if you are feeling overwhelmed and stressed, you may be more likely to snap at someone or become irritable. By recognizing and labeling these emotions, you can communicate your needs to your partner or friend, and they can offer support or help you find ways to cope with your stress.

In addition to improving your self-awareness and communication skills, learning to recognize and label your emotions can also help you make better decisions. When you can identify and name your emotions, you can take them into account when considering different options or making choices. This can help you make more thoughtful and rational decisions, rather than being swayed by impulsive or reactive emotions.

For example, if you are feeling anxious about a presentation you are giving at work, you may be more likely to make impulsive decisions or avoid the presentation altogether. By recognizing and labeling this emotion, you can take a step back and consider whether this is the best course of action. You may choose to practice your presentation, seek support from a colleague, or find ways to cope with your anxiety.

Learning to recognize and label your emotions can also be beneficial for managing stress and improving your overall well-being. When you can identify and name your emotions, you can better understand what is causing them and find healthy ways to cope with them. This can help you manage stress and lead a more fulfilling life.

For example, if you are feeling overwhelmed and stressed, you may be more likely to engage in unhealthy behaviors such as overeating or drinking alcohol to cope. By recognizing and labeling these emotions, you can find healthier ways to cope with stress, such as exercising, practicing mindfulness, or talking to a friend or therapist.

There are several ways you can learn to recognize and label your emotions, including:

- **Paying attention to your body:** Your body can give you clues about how you are feeling. For example, if you are feeling anxious, you may notice physical symptoms such as a racing heart or sweaty palms. Paying attention to these physical cues can help you identify and label your emotions.
- **Using emotion words:** Many words can describe different emotions, such as happy, sad, angry, anxious, and excited. By familiarizing yourself with these words and using them to describe your emotions, you can better recognize and label them.
- **Reflecting on your thoughts and feelings**: Taking the time to reflect on your thoughts and feelings can help you gain insight into why you are feeling a certain way. This can help you identify and label your emotions more accurately.

- **Journaling:** Writing down your thoughts and feelings in a journal can help you better understand and process them. This can be especially helpful if you are struggling to identify or label your emotions.

Learning to recognize and label your emotions is an important skill that can benefit you in many areas of your life. It can help you understand yourself better, communicate more effectively with others, and make better decisions. It can also help you manage stress and lead a more fulfilling life. While it may take time and practice to become proficient in recognizing and labeling your emotions, it is a skill that can have a positive impact on your life.

The role of mindfulness in understanding your emotions

Mindfulness is a mental state achieved by focusing one's awareness on the present moment, while calmly acknowledging and accepting one's feelings, thoughts, and bodily sensations, used as a therapeutic technique. The practice of mindfulness has gained widespread attention in recent years as a means of managing stress, improving mental and physical well-being, and enhancing the overall quality of life.

One key aspect of mindfulness is understanding and managing one's emotions. Emotions are a natural and important part of being human, and they play a crucial role in our decision-making and behavior. However, emotions can also be overwhelming and lead to negative outcomes if not properly managed. This is where mindfulness comes in. By cultivating mindfulness, individuals can learn to become more aware of their emotions as they arise, without getting carried away by them.

One way that mindfulness helps in understanding emotions is by providing a space for non-judgmental observation. When we are mindful, we can observe our emotions without reacting to them or trying to suppress them. This allows us to get a better understanding of what our emotions are telling us and how they are affecting us.

For example, let's say that you are feeling angry about something that happened at work. If you are not mindful, you might immediately react to this emotion by lashing out at a colleague or engaging in some other behavior that you later regret. However, if you can practice mindfulness, you might instead take a step back and observe the emotion without reacting to it. This might involve acknowledging that you are feeling angry, identifying the cause of the emotion, and examining the physical sensations that come along with it. By doing so, you can get a better understanding of what is driving your anger and how it is affecting you.

Another way that mindfulness can help in understanding emotions is by promoting emotional regulation. Emotional regulation refers to the ability to manage and healthily control one's emotions.

When we are mindful, we are better able to regulate our emotions because we are more aware of them as they arise. This can help us to avoid getting carried away by negative emotions and to respond to them more healthily and adaptively.

For example, let's say that you are feeling anxious about an upcoming presentation at work. If you are not mindful, you might become overwhelmed by this anxiety and start to feel panicked. However, if you can practice mindfulness, you might instead take a step back and observe the emotion without getting carried away by it. This might involve acknowledging that you are feeling anxious, identifying the cause of the anxiety, and examining the physical sensations that come along with it. By doing so, you can better manage your anxiety and respond to it more healthily and adaptively.

In addition to promoting emotional awareness and regulation, mindfulness can also help individuals to develop greater emotional intelligence. Emotional intelligence refers to the ability to recognize and understand one's own emotions, as well as the emotions of others. By cultivating mindfulness, individuals can become more attuned to their own emotions and the emotions of others, which can enhance their ability to communicate and interact with others in a more effective and empathetic way.

For example, let's say that you are in a meeting at work and you notice that one of your colleagues is feeling frustrated. If you are not mindful, you might not pick up on this emotion and might not know how to respond. However, if you can practice mindfulness, you might instead take a step back and observe the emotion without reacting to it. This might involve acknowledging that your colleague is feeling frustrated, identifying the cause of the frustration, and examining the physical sensations that come along with it. By doing so, you can better understand your colleague's emotional state and respond to it in a more appropriate and supportive way.

All in all, mindfulness can be a powerful tool for understanding and managing our emotions. By cultivating mindfulness, individuals can become more aware of their emotions as they arise, without getting carried away by them. They can also learn to regulate their emotions healthily and develop greater emotional intelligence. With these skills, individuals can gain a better understanding of their emotions and how they are affecting them, as well as interact with others in a more effective and empathetic way.

CHAPTER III.

Managing Your Emotions

Emotions are a normal and necessary part of the human experience. They help us navigate the world and make decisions, and they can also serve as indicators of our needs and values. However, when emotions become overwhelming or difficult to manage, they can have negative consequences on our mental and physical health, as well as our relationships and daily functioning.

Managing emotions effectively is an important skill that can help us live happier, healthier, and more fulfilling lives.

Here are some Strategies for managing your Emotions:

1. Identify and label your emotions: One of the first steps in managing your emotions is being able to recognize and name them. This can help you better understand your feelings and the reasons behind them. Try to describe your emotions in specific and concrete terms, rather than using vague or general language. For example, instead of saying "I feel bad," try to identify more specific emotions such as "I feel frustrated," "I feel anxious," or "I feel sad."

2. Practice self-awareness: To manage your emotions effectively, it's important to be aware of your thoughts, feelings, and behaviors. This can help you identify patterns and triggers that may be contributing to negative emotions. Take time to reflect on your experiences and pay attention to your emotions throughout the day.

3. Use deep breathing and other relaxation techniques: Deep breathing and other relaxation techniques, such as progressive muscle relaxation or visualization, can help calm the body and mind when you're feeling overwhelmed or anxious. Try taking a few deep breaths, focusing on the sensation of the air entering and leaving your body. You can also try tensing and relaxing specific muscle groups, or picturing a peaceful place in your mind.

4. Engage in physical activity: Physical activity can help reduce stress and improve your overall mood. Whether it's going for a walk, hitting the gym, or participating in a sport, finding ways to move your body can be a powerful tool for managing your emotions.

5. Seek support: It can be helpful to talk to someone about your emotions, whether it's a friend, family member, or mental health professional. Sharing your thoughts and feelings with someone you trust can help you process your emotions and gain perspective.

6. Practice gratitude: Focusing on the things you're grateful for can help shift your focus away from negative emotions and towards the positive. Take time each day to think about and write down things you're grateful for, no matter how small.

7. Engage in activities that bring you joy: Doing activities that bring you pleasure and fulfillment can help lift your mood and improve your overall well-being. Find activities that bring you joy and make time for them in your schedule.

8. Set boundaries: Setting healthy boundaries can help protect your emotional well-being. This means learning to say no when you need to and making sure you have enough time and energy for your own needs and priorities.

9. Practice forgiveness: Holding onto grudges and resentment can take a toll on your emotional well-being. Try to practice forgiveness, both for others and for yourself. This doesn't mean condoning hurtful behavior, but rather letting go of negative emotions and learning to move forward.

10. Seek professional help: If you're struggling to manage your emotions and they're causing significant distress or impacting your daily functioning, it may be helpful to seek the guidance of a mental health professional. A therapist or counselor can help you develop coping skills and strategies for managing your emotions.

11. Challenge negative thinking: Negative thinking can contribute to negative emotions, such as anxiety and depression. Try to challenge your negative thoughts and replace them with more balanced and realistic thoughts.

12. Take a break: If you're feeling overwhelmed or stressed out, it can help to take a break from the situation and practice self-care. This could mean taking a walk, listening to music, or simply taking a few minutes to yourself.

13. Express your emotions in healthy ways: It's important to express your emotions in healthy ways. This could involve talking to a friend, journaling, or engaging in creative activities. Avoid using unhealthy behaviors to cope, such as substance use, self-harm, or disordered eating.

14. Practice mindfulness: Mindfulness is the practice of being aware of your thoughts, feelings, and sensations in the present moment without judgment. Mindfulness can help you be more aware of your emotions and better able to manage them.

15. Use positive self-talk: Try to be kind to yourself and use positive self-talk. This could mean reminding yourself of your strengths and successes, or simply being kind and compassionate to yourself when you're feeling overwhelmed or down.

16. Learn to compromise: Conflict is an inevitable part of life, and learning to compromise can make it easier to manage your emotions when disagreements arise. Try to be open to other perspectives and communicate your needs.

17. Practice self-care: Self-care is an important part of managing your emotions. Make time for activities that bring you pleasure and fulfillment, whether it's taking a relaxing bath, meditating, or going for a walk in nature.

18. Get enough sleep: Sleep is essential for emotional well-being. Aim for 7-9 hours of quality sleep each night to help manage your emotions and reduce stress.

19. Eat a balanced diet: Eating a healthy, balanced diet can help improve your mood and overall well-being. Incorporate plenty of whole foods, such as fruits, vegetables, and whole grains, and limit processed and sugary foods.

20. Limit or avoid alcohol and drugs: Alcohol and drugs can hurt your emotional health. If you're struggling with substance use, seek help from a mental health professional.

21. Avoid negative people: Being around people who are negative or unsupportive can hurt your emotional well-being. Try to spend time with people who are positive and supportive.

22. Take time for yourself: Make time for yourself each day to rest, relax, and do things you enjoy. This could involve reading a book, taking a hot bath, or simply taking a few minutes to yourself.

23. Learn to recognize your triggers: Identifying your triggers can help you better understand your emotions and develop strategies for managing them. Pay attention to your body and environment when you're feeling overwhelmed or upset, and try to identify patterns or triggers that may be contributing to your emotions.

24. Develop problem-solving skills: Developing problem-solving skills can help you manage your emotions in difficult situations. This could involve brainstorming and exploring different solutions, or seeking advice from someone you trust.

25. Challenge yourself: Pushing yourself outside of your comfort zone can help you build self-confidence and resilience. This could involve taking on a new challenge or learning a new skill.

26. Use humor to your advantage: Humor can be a powerful tool for managing emotions. Laughter can help lighten the mood, even in difficult situations.

27. Take a time-out: If you're feeling overwhelmed or frustrated, taking a time-out can help you calm down and gain perspective. Find a quiet space, take a few deep breaths, and focus on calming yourself down.

28. Prioritize your tasks: Prioritizing your tasks can help reduce stress and anxiety. Make a list of tasks you need to complete and focus on the most important ones first.

29. Don't be afraid to ask for help: Asking for help is a sign of strength, not weakness. If you're struggling to manage your emotions, don't hesitate to reach out to a friend, family member, or mental health professional for support.

30. Write it down: Writing down your thoughts and feelings can help you better understand and manage your emotions. Try to be as specific as possible when describing your emotions, and focus on the positives as well as the negatives.

Managing your emotions can be a challenging process. It takes time and practice to develop effective strategies for managing emotions, so don't be too hard on yourself. Take time to reflect on your experiences and make time for activities that bring you joy and fulfillment. Remember that you have the power to choose how you respond to your emotions. With practice and patience, you can learn to better manage your emotions and live a more fulfilling and balanced life.

Strategies for regulating your emotions

Regulating your emotions can be a challenging task, but it is an important skill to have to lead a healthy and fulfilling life. Emotions are a natural part of being human, and they serve a variety of important functions. They can motivate us to take action, communicate our feelings and needs to others, and help us to understand and make sense of the world around us. However, when our emotions become overwhelming or difficult to manage, they can interfere with our ability to think, make good decisions, and function effectively in our daily lives.

There are several strategies Several strategies can

These strategies can be divided into three main categories: Cognitive strategies, Behavioral strategies, and Emotional strategies. Let's take a closer look at each of these categories and some specific strategies within each one:

COGNITIVE STRATEGIES:

Cognitive strategies involve changing the way you think about a situation or emotion to better manage it. Here are a few examples:

Reframing: This involves looking at a situation from a different perspective to see it in a more positive light. For example, instead of thinking "I'll never be able to do this," you could reframe the thought to "I may struggle at first, but I can learn and improve with practice."

Challenging negative thoughts: When we have negative thoughts, they can spiral and lead to negative emotions. It can be helpful to examine the evidence for and against these thoughts and to come up with more balanced, realistic alternatives. For example, if you have the thought "I'm a failure," you might challenge this thought by considering specific examples of successes you've had in the past.

Mindfulness: This involves paying attention to the present moment in a non-judgmental way. When we're mindful, we're able to observe our thoughts and emotions without getting caught up in them. This can help us to become more aware of our emotions and the triggers that lead to them, which can give us more control over how we respond.

BEHAVIORAL STRATEGIES:

Behavioral strategies involve changing your actions or behaviors to better manage your emotions. Some examples include:

Taking a break: When we're feeling overwhelmed or stressed, it can be helpful to step back and take a break. This could involve going for a walk, taking a few deep breaths, or finding a quiet place to sit and relax. Taking a break can allow us to regroup and refocus, which can make it easier to manage our emotions.

Exercise: Regular physical activity has been shown to improve mood and reduce stress. Even just a few minutes of moderate exercise can be enough to make a difference.

Problem-solving: When we're faced with a challenge or a difficult emotion, it can be helpful to take a step back and try to identify the problem and possible solutions. By breaking the problem down into smaller pieces, we can more easily identify concrete steps we can take to address it.

EMOTIONAL STRATEGIES:

Emotional strategies involve directly addressing and managing our emotions. Some examples include:

Self-compassion: This involves being kind and understanding towards ourselves when we're struggling or feeling negative emotions. Research has shown that self-compassion can help to reduce negative emotions and increase well-being.

Emotional expression: When we're feeling overwhelmed by our emotions, it can be helpful to express them healthily. This could involve talking to a trusted friend or family member, journaling, or participating in a creative outlet such as art or music.

Relaxation techniques: There are a variety of relaxation techniques that can help manage intense emotions. These can include deep breathing, progressive muscle relaxation, guided visualization, and mindfulness meditation.

These are just a few of the strategies that can help regulate your emotions. It's important to find the strategies that work best for you and practice them regularly. This will help you to become more aware of your emotions and better able to manage them healthily.

While cognitive, behavioral, and emotional strategies can help manage emotions, it's also important to address any underlying issues that may be contributing to your emotional struggles. If you're struggling with intense or persistent negative emotions, it can be helpful to talk to a mental health professional who can help you to identify and address the root cause of your distress. With the right support and guidance, you can learn to better manage your emotions and lead a more fulfilling life.

The benefits of Emotional Intelligence

Emotional intelligence, also known as emotional quotient (EQ), is the ability to recognize and understand one's own emotions and the emotions of others, and to use this awareness to manage one's behavior and relationships effectively. It involves the ability to perceive, express, understand, and regulate emotions. Emotional intelligence is often referred to as a key component of overall intelligence, as it plays a crucial role in how we navigate and interact with the world around us.

There are numerous benefits to developing high emotional intelligence.

Here are some of the most significant ones:

1. **Improved communication and relationship skills:** People with high emotional intelligence can effectively communicate their own emotions and understand the emotions of others. This allows them to better connect with others and build strong relationships. They can use this understanding to resolve conflicts and manage difficult situations more effectively.

2. **Enhanced decision-making and problem-solving abilities:** Emotional intelligence enables individuals to consider their own emotions and the emotions of others when making decisions and solving problems. This allows them to approach challenges and tasks more rationally and thoughtfully, rather than being swayed by their emotions alone.

3. **Increased resilience and adaptability:** People with high emotional intelligence are better able to cope with stress and setbacks, as they can recognize and healthily manage their own emotions. They are also more adaptable, as they can understand and navigate the emotions of others in a variety of situations.

4. Improved leadership skills: Leaders with high emotional intelligence can effectively communicate and connect with their team members, which can lead to increased productivity and satisfaction among team members. They are also able to recognize and address conflicts within the team in a healthy manner, which helps to create a positive work environment.

5. Greater overall well-being: Developing high emotional intelligence can lead to increased self-awareness, self-regulation, and overall well-being. It allows individuals to better understand and manage their own emotions, which can lead to increased happiness and reduced stress.

6. Higher levels of empathy: People with high emotional intelligence can better understand and empathize with the emotions of others, which can lead to more meaningful connections and relationships. This can also improve their ability to help others in difficult situations and provide more effective support.

7. Improved mental health: Developing emotional intelligence can help to reduce stress, anxiety, and depression, as individuals are better able to understand and manage their own emotions. It can also increase feelings of self-worth and confidence, which can lead to improved mental health.

8. Increased productivity: People with high emotional intelligence can more effectively prioritize tasks and complete them promptly. This can lead to increased productivity, as well as greater job satisfaction.

9. Enhanced creativity: Developing emotional intelligence can help to increase creativity and innovation, as individuals are better able to understand their own emotions and the emotions of others. This can help to inspire more creative solutions to problems and lead to more productive brainstorming sessions.

10. Better performance in the workplace: People with high emotional intelligence are better able to work effectively with their colleagues, manage stress, and stay focused on tasks. This can lead to improved job performance and increased job satisfaction.

11. Increased satisfaction in personal relationships: People with high emotional intelligence are better able to understand and empathize with the emotions of others, which can lead to stronger connections and relationships. This can lead to increased satisfaction in all types of personal relationships.

12. Improved ability to handle challenging situations: Developing emotional intelligence can help individuals to approach challenging situations more effectively. They can better recognize and manage their own emotions, as well as the emotions of others, which can lead to more successful outcomes.

13. Increased self-confidence: Developing emotional intelligence can increase self-confidence, as individuals are better able to understand and manage their own emotions. This can lead to better performance in all areas of life and improved overall well-being.

14. Improved ability to influence others: People with high emotional intelligence are better able to recognize and understand the emotions of others, which can help them to effectively influence and persuade others. This can be beneficial in both personal and professional settings.

15. Increased ability to handle change: Developing emotional intelligence can help individuals to better cope with change and transitions. They are better able to recognize and manage their own emotions, as well as the emotions of others, which can lead to more successful outcomes.

16. Improved ability to manage stress: People with high emotional intelligence are better able to recognize and manage their own emotions, as well as the emotions of others. This can help to reduce stress and lead to improved health and well-being.

17. Increased ability to motivate oneself: Developing emotional intelligence can help individuals to better understand their own emotions and the emotions of others. This can lead to increased motivation and improved performance in all areas of life.

18. Increased ability to recognize and take advantage of opportunities: People with high emotional intelligence are better able to recognize and take advantage of opportunities. They are better able to manage their own emotions and the emotions of others, which can lead to more successful outcomes.

19. Improved ability to build successful teams: Leaders with high emotional intelligence are better able to understand and manage the emotions of their team members. This can lead to increased productivity, collaboration, and satisfaction among team members.

20. Increased ability to make ethical decisions: People with high emotional intelligence are better able to recognize and understand the emotions of others, which can help them to make more ethical decisions. This can lead to improved relationships and better overall outcomes.

Emotional intelligence can be developed and improved upon throughout one's lifetime. Some ways to do this include:

1. Being self-aware: This involves recognizing and understanding one's own emotions, as well as their triggers and effects.

2. Managing emotions: This involves being able to regulate one's own emotions and healthily respond to them.

3. Motivating oneself: This involves being able to use one's emotions to drive oneself towards a goal or task.

4. Recognizing and understanding the emotions of others: This involves being able to accurately perceive and understand the emotions of others, and respond to them in a considerate and appropriate way.

5. Managing relationships: This involves being able to effectively communicate and connect with others, and use this understanding to build and maintain healthy relationships.

6. Empathy: This involves being able to put oneself in another person's shoes and understand their feelings, perspectives, and needs.

7. Decision-making: This involves being able to use one's emotional intelligence to make sound decisions.

8. Problem-solving: This involves being able to take an analytical approach and use one's emotional intelligence to think through problems and come up with solutions.

9. Self-regulation: This involves being able to control one's impulses, manage stress, and remain calm in difficult situations.

10. Developing social skills: This involves being able to build trust, create positive connections, and foster collaboration among diverse groups.

11. Self-reflection: This involves being able to take a step back and objectively assess one's own emotions and actions.

12. Stress management: This involves being able to identify and manage sources of stress to maintain a healthy balance.

13. Creative problem solving: This involves being able to take a creative approach to solve problems and coming up with innovative solutions.

14. Communication: This involves being able to effectively communicate one's thoughts and feelings in a way that is clear and respectful.

15. Conflict resolution: This involves being able to take an assertive approach and use one's emotional intelligence to resolve conflicts constructively.

16. Listening: This involves being able to actively listen to others and pay close attention to their words and body language.

17. Self-care: This involves being able to take care of oneself and practice self-care to maintain emotional balance.

18. Self-esteem: This involves being able to have a positive outlook and develop a healthy sense of self-worth.

19. Adaptability: This involves being able to adjust and adapt to different situations and environments.

20. Optimism: This involves being able to maintain a hopeful and positive attitude despite difficult circumstances.

Coping with Negative Emotions

Negative emotions, such as sadness, anger, fear, and guilt, are a normal and natural part of life. Everyone experiences negative emotions at some point, and they can serve as important signals that something in our lives is not right or needs to be addressed. However, when negative emotions become overwhelming or chronic, they can take a toll on our mental and physical health, relationships, and overall well-being.

Dealing with negative emotions can be challenging, but many strategies and techniques can help us cope with and healthily manage these feelings. Here are sips oping with nee emotions:

1. **Acne and accept yoAcnetionsconcretions**ortant to recogAcnend validate your emotions, rather than trying to ignore or suppress them. Acknowledge that it is okay to

feel negative emotions, and try to sit with them for a while rather than immediately trying to change or fix them.

2. **Practice self-care:** Taking care of yourself is crucial for managing negative emotions. This can include activities such as getting enough sleep, eating well, exercising regularly, and engaging in hobbies or activities that you enjoy.
3. **Use relaxation techniques:** Techniques such as deep breathing, meditation, and progressive muscle relaxation can help reduce stress and manage negative emotions.
4. **Connect with others:** Seeking social support and connection with others can help us feel less alone and give us a sense of perspective. Sharing our feelings with trusted friends or loved ones can also help us process and make sense of our emotions.
5. **Practice gratitude:** Focusing on the things that you are grateful for can help shift your perspective and shift your focus away from negative emotions.
6. **Seek professional help:** If you are struggling to cope with negative emotions on your own, it may be helpful to seek the support of a mental health professional, such as a therapist or counselor.
7. **Use positive self-talk:** Our inner dialogue can have a powerful influence on our emotions. Try to replace negative self-talk with more positive and realistic thoughts.

8. **Engage in activities that bring you joy:** Doing things that bring you joy and meaning can help counteract negative emotions and improve your overall well-being.
9. **Practice forgiveness:** Forgiveness can be difficult, but it can also be a powerful tool for healing and moving on from negative emotions.
10. **Find healthy ways to cope with stress:** Stress can contribute to negative emotions, so finding healthy ways to manage stress, such as through exercise or mindfulness, can help cope with negative emotions.

It is important to remember that coping with negative emotions is a process, and it may take time and effort to find the strategies that work best for you. It is also okay to not have all the answers and to ask for help when you need it.

Some additional strategies for coping with negative emotions include:

- Engaging in activities that promote mindfulness, such as yoga or journaling
- Seeking out positive role models or mentors
- Using visualization or positive imagery to reframe negative thoughts
- Trying to find the humor in difficult situations
- Engaging in creative activities, such as art or music

- Volunteering or helping others
- Seeking out spiritual or religious practices that provide comfort and meaningIt is important to remember that everyone is different and what works for one person may not work for another. It is okay to try out different strategies and see what works best for you.

Generally, negative emotions are a normal and natural part of life, and it is important to find healthy ways to cope with and manage these feelings. Acknowledging and accepting your emotions, practicing self-care, using relaxation techniques, connecting with others, practicing gratitude and forgiveness, and engaging in activities that bring you joy are all strategies that can help you cope with negative emotions. If you are struggling to cope on your own, it can be helpful to seek the support of a mental health professional. Everyone is different and it may take some time and effort to find the strategies that work best for you.

CHAPTER IV.

Building Emotional Resilience

What is emotional resilience and how can it be developed?

Emotional resilience is the ability to bounce back from setbacks, challenges, and difficult emotions. It is an important skill to have as it helps us to cope with the ups and downs of life and to maintain a sense of well-being even in the face of adversity. Emotional resilience is an important quality to have in life, as it enables individuals to handle difficult situations and emotions effectively, rather than becoming overwhelmed or defeated by them. It can also help people to build stronger relationships, as it allows them to communicate and express their emotions effectively, rather than becoming reactive or shutting down. Building emotional resilience is not something that happens overnight, rather it is a process that takes time and effort.

Here are some strategies you can use to build emotional resilience:

1. Identify and acknowledge your emotions: A key part of emotional resilience is being able to recognize and understand your own emotions. This can help you to manage your emotions and to respond to challenges healthily. When you are feeling overwhelmed or upset, take a moment to pause and reflect on what you are feeling. This can help you to better understand your emotions and to find ways to cope with them.

2. Practice mindfulness: Mindfulness is the practice of focusing on the present moment and being aware of your thoughts and feelings without judgment. It can help you to be more aware of your emotions and to respond to them healthily. To practice mindfulness, try to focus on your breath, your body, and your surroundings. You can also try mindfulness exercises, such as deep breathing or meditation, to help you become more aware of your emotions.

3. Develop a positive outlook: A positive outlook can help you to bounce back from setbacks and to maintain a sense of hope and optimism even in the face of adversity. Try to focus on the things in your life that are going well, and practice gratitude by expressing appreciation for the good things in your life. You can also try to reframe negative thoughts into more positive ones and find the silver lining in difficult situations.

4. Cultivate social support: Having supportive relationships with friends and loved ones can provide a sense of connection and belonging, which can help to build emotional resilience. It can also be helpful to have someone to talk to when you are feeling overwhelmed or struggling with difficult emotions. Reach out to people you trust and let them know when you need support.

5. Set healthy boundaries: It is important to set boundaries with people to maintain a sense of control and balance in your life. This can help to prevent you from feeling overwhelmed and overburdened. Identify what is important to you and communicate your needs clearly to those around you.

6. Take care of your body: Taking care of your physical health is an important part of building emotional resilience. Eating a balanced diet, getting regular exercise, and getting enough sleep can help to keep your body and mind strong.

7. Practice self-care: Self-care is the practice of taking time to rest, relax, and recharge. This can help to reduce stress and to maintain a sense of balance and well-being. Make sure to take time for yourself each day to do something that you enjoy and to nurture your body, mind, and spirit.

8. Challenge yourself: Taking on new challenges and pushing yourself out of your comfort zone can help to build emotional resilience. Taking on a new project at work, learning a new skill, or trying something new can help to boost your confidence and to give you a sense of accomplishment.

9. Develop problem-solving skills: Problem-solving is an important skill to have when it comes to dealing with difficult emotions and challenging situations. Take some time to think about the problem and brainstorm potential solutions. This can help you to gain perspective and to come up with creative solutions.

10. Accept your limitations: It is important to accept that you are not perfect and that you cannot control everything in your life. Accepting your limitations can help to reduce stress and to give you a sense of peace.

11. Let go of the past: Holding onto the past can be a barrier to emotional resilience. It can be helpful to practice forgiveness and to let go of negative emotions from past experiences.

12. Practice self-compassion: Self-compassion is the practice of being kind and understanding towards yourself when things don't go as planned. Instead of being hard on yourself, practice self-compassion and recognize that mistakes are part of the learning process.

13. Engage in meaningful activities: Doing activities that you find meaningful and enjoyable can help to boost your mood and to give you a sense of purpose. This can help to reduce stress and to give you a sense of satisfaction.

14. Develop a sense of humor: Having a sense of humor can help to lighten the mood and to put things into perspective. Laughing and having fun can help to reduce stress and to give you a sense of joy and contentment.

15. Find a mentor: A mentor can provide valuable guidance and support. Find someone you trust and can talk to about your challenges and successes. This can help to provide perspective and to give you motivation and inspiration.

16. Develop coping strategies: Developing healthy coping strategies can help to reduce stress and to manage difficult emotions healthily. Examples of healthy coping strategies include deep breathing, positive self-talk, and engaging in physical activity.

17. Reach out for help: When you are feeling overwhelmed, it is important to reach out for help. Talking to a trusted friend, family member, or mental health professional can help to provide support and to give you the tools to cope.

18. Take action: Taking action can help to give you a sense of control and to reduce feelings of helplessness. Identify what needs to be done and break it down into manageable tasks. Taking small steps can help to reduce stress and to give you a sense of accomplishment.

19. Practice gratitude: Gratitude is the practice of expressing appreciation for the good things in your life. Taking time to appreciate the good things in your life can help to reduce stress and to give you a sense of contentment.

20. Find joy in the present moment: Taking time to appreciate the present moment can help to reduce stress and to give you a sense of peace. Find joy in the little things in life, such as spending time with loved ones or taking a walk in nature.

The role of self-care in building emotional resilience

Self-care is a term that refers to the actions an individual takes to care for their physical, mental, and emotional health. It can include activities such as exercise, eating a balanced diet, getting enough sleep, practicing relaxation techniques, and seeking social support. Self-care is often thought of as a means of maintaining good health, but it can also play a crucial role in building emotional resilience.

Emotional resilience is the ability to effectively cope with and recover from stress, adversity, and challenges. It involves being able to bounce back from difficult experiences and maintain a positive outlook, even in the face of adversity. Building emotional resilience requires a combination of personal and social resources, including a strong sense of self-worth, effective coping skills, and a supportive network of family and friends.

Self-care can be a powerful tool for building emotional resilience because it helps individuals to maintain a sense of balance and control in their lives. When we are under stress or facing difficult circumstances, it can be easy to neglect our own needs and forget to take care of ourselves. This can lead to physical and emotional exhaustion, which can make it even harder to cope with challenges. By making self-care a priority, we can build up our physical and emotional resources and be better equipped to handle difficult situations.

Here are some specific ways that self-care can help to build emotional resilience:

1. **Reducing stress:** Self-care activities can help to reduce stress by promoting relaxation and relaxation techniques such as deep breathing, progressive muscle relaxation, and mindfulness meditation can help to reduce stress and improve emotional well-being.

2. **Improving physical health:** Taking care of our physical health is an important aspect of self-care. Exercise, healthy eating, and getting enough sleep can all contribute to better physical health, which in turn can improve our emotional well-being and resilience.

3. **Enhancing self-esteem:** Self-care can help to improve self-esteem by promoting a sense of self-worth and competence. When we take the time to care for ourselves, it can make us feel more capable and confident in our ability to handle life's challenges.

4. **Building social connections:** Social connections are a key component of emotional resilience. Self-care can involve seeking support from friends, family, or a support group, which can help to

build a sense of belonging and provide a source of strength and encouragement.

5. Developing coping skills: Self-care can also involve learning and practicing effective coping skills, such as problem-solving, communication, and stress management techniques. These skills can help us to better handle difficult situations and emotions, and increase our emotional resilience.

6. Practicing self-compassion: Self-care can involve practicing self-compassion, which involves treating ourselves with kindness and understanding. Self-compassion can help to reduce feelings of guilt and shame and increase feelings of self-worth and acceptance.

7. Engaging in creative activities: Creative activities such as art, music, and writing can be a great way to express our emotions and gain insight into our thoughts and feelings. Taking part in creative activities can help to reduce stress and provide a sense of satisfaction.

8. Developing mindfulness: Mindfulness is the practice of being present in the moment and aware of our thoughts and feelings without judgment. Practicing mindfulness can help to reduce stress and improve our ability to cope with difficult emotions.

9. Setting boundaries: Self-care can involve setting boundaries to protect our physical and emotional health. Setting boundaries can help to prevent us from becoming overwhelmed and exhausted by the demands of others and can help to maintain balance and emotional stability.

10. Practicing gratitude: Practicing gratitude can help to shift our perspective and focus on the positive aspects of our lives. Taking time to appreciate the good things in life can help to reduce stress and improve our emotional resilience.

11. Nurturing spiritual connection: Taking time to connect with our spiritual side can help to provide us with a sense of purpose and meaning, which can help to improve our emotional resilience.

12. Making time for leisure: Taking time to do activities that we enjoy, such as reading, listening to music, or spending time outdoors, can help to reduce stress and provide a sense of relaxation and enjoyment.

13. Engaging in physical activities: Engaging in physical activities such as walking, jogging, or yoga can help to reduce stress and boost our mood.

14. Seeking professional help: Seeking help from a professional, such as a therapist or counselor, can help to identify and address underlying issues that can contribute to stress and emotional distress.

15. Practicing assertiveness: Being assertive can help to protect our emotional health by allowing us to express our thoughts and feelings clearly and respectfully.

16. Taking time for yourself: Taking time for yourself to relax and unwind can help to reduce stress and prevent us from becoming overwhelmed.

17. Taking breaks from technology: Taking breaks from technology can help to reduce stress and improve our emotional well-being.

18. Practicing positive self-talk: Practicing positive self-talk can help to reduce stress and improve our self-esteem.

19. Having fun: Taking time to do activities that we enjoy, such as going to the movies or playing sports, can help to reduce stress and provide a sense of fun and relaxation.

20. Making time for nature: Taking time to connect with nature can help to reduce stress and improve our emotional resilience...

Incorporating self-care into our daily lives can be challenging, especially when we are busy or under a lot of stress. However, making self-care a priority can pay off in the long run by helping us to build emotional resilience and better cope with life's challenges. Some strategies for making self-care a priority include setting aside specific times for self-care activities, enlisting the support of friends and family, and finding activities that are enjoyable and nourishing.

It is important to note that self-care is not a one-size-fits-all solution, and what works for one person may not work for another. It is important to experiment with different self-care activities and find what works best for you. Some people may find that physical activities, such as exercise or yoga, are helpful for stress relief, while others may prefer activities that involve more solitude and reflection, such as journaling or art therapy. The key is to find activities that nourish and support your physical, mental, and emotional well-being.

Strategies for developing a positive mindset

Developing a positive mindset can have a significant impact on your life and overall well-being. It can help you to cope with stress, overcome challenges, and achieve your goals.

Here are some Strategies you can use to develop a positive mindset:

1. **Practice gratitude:** Focusing on the things you are grateful for can help to shift your perspective and cultivate a more positive outlook. Try keeping a gratitude journal where you write down three things you are grateful for each day. You

can also practice expressing gratitude to others by thanking them for their contributions and support.

2. **Engage in positive self-talk:** The way you speak to yourself can have a big impact on your mindset. Instead of engaging in negative self-talk or putting yourself down, try to speak to yourself with kindness and compassion. Acknowledge your accomplishments and successes, and remind yourself of your strengths and abilities.
3. **Set achievable goals:** Setting and achieving goals can help to build self-confidence and a sense of accomplishment, which can contribute to a positive mindset. Make sure to set goals that are realistic and achievable, and break them down into smaller, more manageable steps. This can help to reduce the feeling of being overwhelmed and increase your chances of success.
4. **Surround yourself with positive influences:** The people you spend time with can have a big impact on your mindset. Surround yourself with positive, supportive people who lift you and encourage you to be your best self. Avoid negative influences or toxic relationships that drain your energy and bring you down.
5. **Engage in activities that bring you joy:** Doing things that bring you joy and fulfillment can help to boost your mood and cultivate a more positive mindset. This could be anything from hobbies, to spending time with loved ones,

to volunteering for a cause you care about. Make time for activities that bring you happiness and a sense of purpose.

6. **Learn to reframe negative thoughts:** It's natural to have negative thoughts from time to time, but it's important to learn how to reframe them in a more positive light. Instead of dwelling on the negative aspects of a situation, try to focus on the positive aspects or what you can learn from the experience. This can help to shift your perspective and cultivate a more positive mindset.
7. **Practice mindfulness:** Mindfulness is the practice of being present in the moment and paying attention to your thoughts and feelings without judgment. It can help to increase awareness and reduce stress, which can contribute to a more positive mindset. There are many ways to practice mindfulness, such as through meditation, yoga, or simply taking a few deep breaths and focusing on the present moment.
8. **Take care of your physical well-being:** Your physical well-being can have a big impact on your mindset. Make sure to get enough sleep, eat a healthy diet, and engage in regular physical activity. These habits can help to improve your energy levels, boost your mood, and cultivate a more positive mindset.
9. **Seek support when needed:** It's okay to ask for help when you need it. If you're struggling with negative thoughts or

emotions, consider seeking support from a mental health professional, a trusted friend or family member, or a support group. Talking to someone about what you're going through can help to alleviate stress and improve your overall well-being.

By incorporating these strategies into your daily life, you can work to develop a more positive mindset and improve your overall well-being. Remember that it's a process and it may take time, but with consistent effort, you can cultivate a more positive outlook and approach to life.

Developing a positive mindset starts with being mindful of your thoughts and feelings. Pay attention to the way you talk to yourself and try to reframe negative thoughts in a more positive light. Acknowledge your accomplishments and successes, and surround yourself with positive influences. Make time for activities that bring you joy and fulfillment, and take care of your physical well-being. Set achievable goals that are realistic and achievable, and practice gratitude and self-compassion. If you're struggling, don't be afraid to seek support. With consistent effort and practice, you can develop a more positive mindset and create a life that you love.

CHAPTER V.

Exploring Your Emotional Triggers

Identifying and understanding your emotional triggers

Emotional triggers can be defined as an event or situation that causes a person to have an emotional reaction, usually one that is negative or uncomfortable. There are many different types of emotional triggers, such as stress, fear, anger, sadness, and even joy. It is important to understand how and why these triggers occur to better manage them. Identifying and understanding your emotional triggers can help you to respond more positively and effectively when faced with difficult situations.

What are emotional triggers?

An emotional trigger is an event or situation that causes a person to have an emotional reaction. It can be something as simple as a certain sound, smell, or sight, or it can be a more complex situation such as a stressful situation at work or an argument with a loved one. Emotional triggers can be either positive or negative, depending on the person and the situation. Positive triggers can help to bring a sense of joy or happiness, while negative triggers can cause feelings of anger, fear, or sadness.

Emotional triggers can be a powerful force in our lives and can be used to help us process and manage our emotions. By recognizing our emotional triggers and learning how to effectively manage them, we can become better equipped to navigate difficult emotional situations and lead healthier happier lives.

What are the different types of emotional triggers?

There are many different types of emotional triggers.

Some of the most common include Stress, Fear, Anger, Sadness, and Joy.

Stress: Stress is a very common emotional trigger that can be triggered by a variety of different situations. It can be caused by work, relationships, finances, or even just day-to-day life. Stress can lead to feelings of anxiety, irritability, and even depression.

When experiencing stress, it is important to recognize it and take steps to reduce it. This could involve taking breaks from work or other activities, engaging in hobbies, exercising, meditating, or talking to a professional. It is also important to practice good self-care and get enough sleep and rest.

There are also lifestyle changes that can help reduce stress, such as eating a healthy diet and avoiding unhealthy habits like smoking and drinking. It is also important to practice positive self-talk and to stay connected with supportive friends and family.

Stress can have negative impacts on our physical and mental health, so it is important to recognize it and take steps to manage it. Taking time to relax and practice self-care is key to reducing stress and improving overall well-being.

Fear: Fear can be triggered by a variety of different situations, such as an upcoming test or a difficult decision. Fear is a natural reaction that helps us to protect ourselves from potential danger. However, if fear is not managed properly, it can lead to feelings of panic or even paralysis.

Fear is an emotion that we all experience at some point in our lives, and it can be triggered by both external and internal stimuli. For example, fear can be triggered by a dangerous situation, such as being in a dark alley alone at night. Fear can also be triggered by our thoughts, such as worrying about an upcoming test or a difficult decision that needs to be made. In either case, fear is a natural reaction that helps us to protect ourselves from potential danger.

However, if fear is not managed properly, it can lead to feelings of panic or even paralysis. In some cases, fear can result in people avoiding any sort of action or decision, even if it is necessary for their safety and well-being. This avoidance can be detrimental to physical, mental, and emotional health.

To manage fear effectively, it is important to understand where it is coming from and to try to break it down into smaller, more manageable pieces. It is also important to take deep breaths and focus on the present moment, rather than on potential future outcomes. Additionally, it is helpful to talk to trusted friends and family members about your fears and to practice calming activities, such as yoga or meditation.

Overall, fear can be a difficult emotion to manage, but with the right tools and techniques, it can be done. Understanding where fear comes from and confronting it can help to reduce its power and make it more manageable.

Anger: Anger is an emotion that is often triggered by feeling threatened or frustrated. It is a natural reaction that is designed to protect us from danger or injustice. However, if left unchecked, it can lead to aggressive behavior or even violence.

When we feel angry, our bodies release stress hormones such as adrenaline and cortisol which can cause physical reactions such as increased heart rate and blood pressure. This can lead to a feeling of tension and a need to act quickly.

Anger can be constructive or destructive. Constructive anger can be used to motivate us to take action, stand up for ourselves or others, and even solve problems. However, destructive anger can lead to aggressive behavior, hurtful words, physical violence, and even long-term consequences.

It is important to recognize when we are feeling angry and to recognize what sparks it. Taking the time to understand the cause of our anger can help us manage it better and allow us to choose a more positive response. It is also important to practice healthy coping strategies such as relaxation techniques, physical activity, or talking to a friend.

Anger is a normal emotion, but it is important to recognize when it is getting out of control. If you find yourself unable to control your anger, it is important to seek help from a mental health professional.

Sadness: Sadness is an emotion that can be triggered by a variety of different situations, such as the loss of a loved one or a breakup. It is a natural reaction that helps us to process our pain and cope with a difficult situation is a feeling of sorrow and despair that can leave us feeling helpless, overwhelmed, and alone.

Sadness can manifest in a variety of ways, both physically and emotionally. Physically, sadness can lead to changes in appetite, sleeping patterns, and energy levels. Emotionally, sadness can lead to feelings of depression, guilt, and hopelessness. It can also cause us to withdraw from our normal activities and social circles.

When we are feeling sad, it is important to acknowledge our feelings and take steps to cope with them. Talking to a trusted friend, participating in activities that bring us joy, and finding ways to express our feelings can all be helpful. Additionally, seeking professional help if needed can be beneficial.

Sadness is often a part of life, but it does not have to define us. By taking steps to cope with sad feelings, we can work through them and find ways to move forward. Although sadness is a normal part of life, it is important to remember that we do not have to be stuck in it forever. With time and effort, we can learn to cope with our sadness and find a way to move forward.

Joy: Joy is an emotion that is triggered by positive experiences, such as success or a happy memory. It is a natural reaction that helps us to appreciate the good things in life and find meaning in our experiences. Joy can be experienced in a variety of ways, including through physical sensations, such as a smile or a hug, or through mental activity, such as a good conversation or a meaningful song. It can also come from a spiritual source, such as a religious experience or a connection with nature.

Joy is an important part of the human experience and it can have a powerful influence on our lives. Joy can bring us peace, contentment, and satisfaction, helping us to feel connected to something greater than ourselves. It can bring us energy and enthusiasm, motivating us to take action and pursue our goals. It can also bring us courage and strength, helping us to face difficult challenges or take risks that may lead to greater rewards.

Joy can also be a tool for healing and growth. When we are feeling joy, we are more likely to be open to learning and growing. We can learn to recognize and appreciate the joy in our lives, allowing ourselves to become more connected with our inner selves. Additionally, joy can help us to build strong relationships with the people and places around us.

Joy is an emotion that can be felt in many different ways, and it can bring us many benefits. It can help us to find peace and contentment, give us energy and enthusiasm, and provide us with the courage and strength that we need to face difficult challenges. Joy can also be a tool for healing and growth, allowing us to become more connected with our inner selves and build strong relationships with the people and places around us.

How can you identify and understand your emotional triggers?

The first step in identifying and understanding your emotional triggers is to become aware of your emotional reactions. Pay attention to how you feel in different situations and try to identify what triggers your emotions. It can be helpful to keep a journal and write down your thoughts and feelings.

Once you have identified your emotional triggers, it is important to understand why they are happening. Ask yourself questions such as: What is the root cause of this emotion? What is the underlying fear or insecurity? What can I do to reduce the stress or fear?

It is also important to remember that emotions are not always rational and that it is okay to feel them. Acknowledge your emotions and try to accept them instead of suppressing or denying them.

How can you manage your emotional triggers?

Once you have identified and understood your emotional triggers, it is important to find ways to manage them.

Here are some tips to help you manage your emotional triggers:

- **Take a break:** Taking a break from the situation or activity that is causing your emotional reaction can help to reduce your stress and emotional intensity.
- **Practice relaxation techniques:** Relaxation techniques such as deep breathing, meditation, and yoga can help to reduce stress and improve your emotional well-being.

- **Exercise:** Exercise can help to reduce stress and boost your mood.
- **Talk to a friend or a therapist:** Talking to a trusted friend or a therapist can help you to process your emotions and find better ways to manage them.
- **Take time for yourself:** Taking time for yourself, such as reading a book or taking a walk, can help to reduce stress and improve your emotional well-being.

The role of past experiences in shaping emotional triggers

We often hear the phrase "you are a product of your past" and this is especially true when it comes to our emotional triggers. The experiences we have had in the past have a major role in shaping our emotional triggers. This is because our emotional triggers are shaped by the memories and experiences we have had. Emotional triggers are reactions to certain events or stimuli that cause us to feel a certain emotion. These triggers can be positive or negative and can be triggered by anything from a familiar smell to a certain phrase. The way we react to these triggers is determined by our past experiences and how we have learned to cope with them.

The past experiences we have had in our lives can have a major influence on how we react to certain triggers. For example, if someone has had a negative experience in the past with a certain type of person or situation, this may cause them to react more strongly to similar situations in the future. This is because the person has learned to associate certain triggers with negative experiences and will be more likely to react negatively to similar triggers in the future. On the other hand, if someone has had a positive experience with the same type of person or situation, they may be more likely to react positively when a similar situation arises.

The way we react to certain triggers can also be shaped by how we were raised. Our parents and other adults in our lives can play an important role in how we respond to certain triggers. If an adult in our life taught us to suppress our emotions or to not react to certain triggers, this can lead us to be more likely to do the same in the future. On the other hand, if an adult in our life taught us to express our emotions or to respond to certain triggers, this can lead us to be more likely to do the same in the future.

Our past experiences can also shape how we interpret certain triggers. For example, if someone has had a negative experience in the past with a certain type of person or situation, this may cause them to interpret similar situations in a more negative light in the future. This is because the person has learned to associate certain triggers with negative experiences and will be more likely to view similar triggers negatively in the future. On the other hand, if someone has had a positive experience with the same type of person or situation, they may be more likely to interpret similar situations in a more positive light in the future.

Our emotional triggers can also be shaped by the relationships we have had in the past. If we have had negative relationships in the past, this can lead us to be more likely to have negative reactions to certain triggers in the future. This is because we have learned to associate certain triggers with negative experiences and will be more likely to react negatively to similar triggers in the future. On the other hand, if we have had positive relationships in the past, this can lead us to be more likely to have positive reactions to certain triggers in the future.

The way we were treated in the past can also have a major influence on our emotional triggers. If we were treated poorly in the past, this can lead us to be more likely to have negative reactions to certain triggers in the future. This is because we have learned to associate certain triggers with negative experiences and will be more likely to react negatively to similar triggers in the future. On the other hand, if we were treated well in the past, this can lead us to be more likely to have positive reactions to certain triggers in the future.

Our past experiences can also influence what triggers us. If we have had negative experiences in the past, this can lead us to be more likely to be triggered by certain triggers in the future. This is because we have learned to associate certain triggers with negative experiences and will be more likely to be triggered by similar triggers in the future. On the other hand, if we have had positive experiences in the past, this can lead us to be more likely to be triggered by certain triggers in the future.

The way we view the world can also be shaped by our past experiences. If we have had negative experiences in the past, this can lead us to be more likely to view the world in a negative light. This is because we have learned to associate certain triggers with negative experiences and will be more likely to view similar triggers negatively in the future. On the other hand, if we have had positive experiences in the past, this can lead us to be more likely to view the world in a more positive light.

Ultimately, past experiences can influence how we cope with certain triggers. If we have had negative experiences in the past, this can lead us to be more likely to cope with certain triggers negatively. This is because we have learned to associate certain triggers with negative experiences and will be more likely to cope with similar triggers negatively in the future. On the other hand, if we have had positive experiences in the past, this can lead us to be more likely to cope with certain triggers more positively.

Overall, our past experiences have a major role in shaping our emotional triggers. The way we view the world, the relationships we have had, the way we were treated, and the way we cope with certain triggers can all be shaped by our past experiences. It is important to be aware of how our past experiences may be influencing our emotional triggers so that we can better understand why we react the way we do to certain triggers in the future.

Strategies for managing and reducing the impact of emotional triggers

Emotional triggers are stimuli that elicit strong emotional responses in individuals. These triggers can be positive or negative, and they can have a significant impact on a person's behavior and decision-making.

Managing and reducing the impact of emotional triggers is an important skill that can help individuals maintain a healthy emotional balance and make more rational decisions.

Here are some strategies that can help manage and reduce the impact of emotional triggers:

1. Identify your emotional triggers: The first step in managing your emotional triggers is to identify what they are. This can be done by paying attention to your thoughts, feelings, and behaviors when you experience strong emotions. You can also try keeping a journal to track your emotional reactions to different stimuli.

2. Practice mindfulness: Mindfulness is a practice that involves paying attention to your present moment experience with an open, curious, and non-judgmental attitude. By practicing mindfulness, you can become more aware of your emotional reactions and learn to respond to them in a more mindful and balanced way.

3. Use self-soothing techniques: Self-soothing techniques are techniques that can help you calm down and manage strong emotions. Some self-soothing techniques include deep breathing, progressive muscle relaxation, and visualizing a peaceful place.

4. Challenge negative thought patterns: Negative thought patterns, such as all-or-nothing thinking and catastrophic thinking, can intensify negative emotions. By learning to challenge and reframe these negative thoughts, you can reduce the impact of emotional triggers.

5. Seek support: Reaching out to friends, family, or a mental health professional can be an effective way to manage and reduce the impact of emotional triggers. These individuals can provide a listening ear, a different perspective, and practical strategies for managing emotions.

6. Use cognitive-behavioral techniques: Cognitive-behavioral techniques are strategies that involve modifying negative thoughts and behaviors that contribute to negative emotions. Examples of cognitive-behavioral techniques include thought records, exposure therapy, and problem-solving skills training.

7. Practice self-care: Taking care of your physical and emotional well-being is important for managing emotional triggers. This can include getting enough sleep, exercising regularly, eating a healthy diet, and engaging in activities that bring you joy and relaxation.

8. Learn relaxation techniques: Relaxation techniques, such as meditation, yoga, or tai chi, can help you manage stress and reduce the impact of emotional triggers. These techniques can help you calm your mind and body and increase your ability to cope with difficult emotions.

9. Seek professional help: If you are struggling to manage your emotional triggers and they are affecting your daily life, it may be helpful to seek professional help. A mental health professional can provide support and guidance in managing your emotions and reducing the impact of emotional triggers.

10. Identify your emotional strengths: Everyone has emotional strengths that can be used to help manage emotional triggers. Identifying and building upon your emotional strengths can help you better recognize and manage your emotional triggers.

11. Learn to recognize emotional patterns: Over time, you may notice patterns in your emotional reactions to certain stimuli.

Recognizing these patterns can help you anticipate and manage your emotional triggers more effectively.

12. Practice self-acceptance: Self-acceptance is the practice of accepting yourself, including your emotions and thoughts. Practicing self-acceptance can help you manage your emotions and reduce the impact of emotional triggers.

13. Cultivate healthy coping skills: Unhealthy coping skills, such as avoiding or numbing emotions, can worsen the impact of emotional triggers. Developing healthy coping skills, such as safely expressing emotions or engaging in activities that help you relax, can help reduce the impact of emotional triggers.

14. Practice gratitude: Practicing gratitude can help shift your focus away from negative emotions and help reduce the impact of emotional triggers. Taking time to appreciate the good in your life can help put things into perspective and reduce the intensity of emotional reactions.

15. Take time for yourself: Making time for yourself can help reduce the impact of emotional triggers. This can be as simple as taking a few minutes each day to do something that you enjoy or spending time with friends and family.

16. Learn to set boundaries: Setting boundaries can help you manage your emotional triggers. This includes setting limits on how much time you spend with certain people or activities and learning to say "no" when necessary.

17. Practice being assertive: Assertiveness is the practice of expressing your needs and feelings clearly and directly. Being assertive can help reduce the impact of emotional triggers by helping you to better communicate your needs and feelings.

18. Stay connected: Staying connected to others can help reduce the impact of emotional triggers. Connecting with friends and family, or participating in social activities can help you manage difficult emotions and reduce the intensity of emotional reactions.

19. Use distraction techniques: Distraction techniques can help manage emotional triggers. Examples of distraction techniques include listening to music, reading a book, or engaging in a hobby.

20. Use positive reframing: Positive reframing is the practice of looking at a situation in a more positive light. This can help reduce the intensity of negative emotions and help manage emotional triggers.

21. Foster positive relationships: Positive relationships can help reduce the impact of emotional triggers. Spending time with supportive people and understanding can help you manage your emotions and reduce the intensity of emotional reactions.

22. Avoid triggers when possible: Avoiding certain situations or people that may trigger strong emotions can help manage emotional triggers. This can help reduce the intensity of your emotional reactions and give you time to practice calming techniques.

23. Practice problem-solving skills: Problem-solving skills can help you manage difficult emotions and reduce the impact of emotional triggers. These skills involve breaking a problem down into smaller parts, generating potential solutions, and evaluating the potential solutions.

24. Get organized: Being organized can help reduce the impact of emotional triggers. This can include organizing your living space, making to-do lists, and setting goals for yourself.

25. Take a break: Taking a break from a situation or activity that is triggering strong emotions can help reduce the intensity of your reactions. This can include taking a few minutes to take some deep breaths or going for a walk to clear your head.

However, managing and reducing the impact of emotional triggers requires a combination of self-awareness, self-care, and effective coping strategies. By identifying your emotional triggers, practicing mindfulness and self-soothing techniques, and seeking support when needed, you can learn to manage and reduce the impact of emotional triggers and maintain a healthy emotional balance.

CHAPTER VI.

Finding Emotional Support

Emotional support is an important aspect of well-being and mental health. It refers to the comfort, encouragement, and validation we receive from others during times of stress, sadness, or difficulty. Emotional support can come from a wide range of sources, including friends, family members, therapists, support groups, and even strangers who offer a kind word or a listening ear.

However, finding emotional support can be challenging, especially in times of crisis or when we feel isolated and alone. This can be especially true for those who struggle with mental health issues, who may feel stigmatized or misunderstood. That's why it's important to seek out sources of emotional support and to make sure that we are connecting with people who can truly understand and empathize with our feelings.

Whether it's through online forums, support groups, counseling, or just talking to a friend, emotional support can be essential for our mental health and well-being. It can help us process our emotions, make sense of our experiences, and feel connected and supported. It can also provide us with valuable insight and help us find healthy ways to cope with difficult situations.

The Importance of social connections in emotional well-being

Human beings are social creatures and have a natural inclination towards social connections. From an evolutionary perspective, the ability to form and maintain social connections was crucial for survival. In the modern world, social connections continue to be an important aspect of human life and are essential for emotional well-being.

Research has shown that people with strong social connections have better physical and mental health, higher levels of happiness and life satisfaction, and lower levels of stress and anxiety. On the other hand, people with weak social connections or who are socially isolated are more prone to mental health issues, such as depression and anxiety, and have a higher risk of physical health problems, such as heart disease and stroke.

There are several reasons why social connections are important for emotional well-being.

1. Social connections provide a sense of belonging and purpose: Belonging to a social group gives people a sense of identity and purpose. It helps individuals feel like they are part of something larger than themselves and that their actions and contributions are meaningful. This sense of purpose and belonging can contribute to feelings of happiness and satisfaction.

2. Social connections provide support and encouragement: Having a strong social network can provide emotional support and encouragement during difficult times. Friends and family members can offer emotional comfort, practical assistance, and a listening ear when you need it. This support can help people cope with stress and adversity, and can improve their emotional well-being.

3. Social connections can provide a sense of security and protection: Having a supportive social network can provide a sense of security and protection. It can give people the confidence to take risks and try new things, knowing that they have a safety net of friends and family to fall back on if things don't go as planned.

4. Social connections can promote healthy behaviors: Having a strong social network can also promote healthy behaviors. For example, friends and family members can encourage and support each other in pursuing healthy lifestyle choices, such as exercising regularly, eating a healthy diet, and not smoking.

5. Social connections can provide a sense of connection and purpose: Having close social connections can provide a sense of connection and purpose, which can be especially important for people who are feeling lonely or isolated. It can give people someone to talk to, share experiences with, and spend time with, which can improve their emotional well-being.

6. Social connections can help people learn and grow: Social connections can provide opportunities to learn and grow. Friends and family members can offer advice and guidance, introduce people to new ideas and experiences, and help them work through difficult situations.

7. Social connections can help foster resilience: Having a strong social network can help people develop resilience, or the ability to cope with and adapt to challenging situations. Friends and family members can provide emotional support, practical assistance, and encouragement during difficult times, which can help people to stay strong and find solutions to their problems.

8. Social connections can help improve self-esteem: Social connections can also help improve self-esteem. Friends and family members can provide compliments, recognition, and appreciation, which can help people to feel valued and appreciated and can boost their self-esteem.

9. Social connections can help people cope with stress and adversity: Having a strong social network can help people cope with stress and adversity. Friends and family members can provide emotional support, practical assistance, and a listening ear when needed, which can help people to feel less overwhelmed and more capable of dealing with difficult situations.

10. Social connections can help people build meaningful relationships: Social connections can also help people build meaningful relationships. Friends and family members can provide companionship, understanding, and empathy, which can help people to cultivate deeper, more meaningful relationships...

There are several ways to strengthen social connections and improve emotional well-being.

Here are ways to strengthen social connections and improve emotional well-being.

1. Make an effort to stay in touch with friends and family: It's easy to get caught up in the busyness of life and let social connections fall by the wayside. Make an effort to stay in touch with friends and family members, even if it's just through a quick phone call or text message.

2. Volunteer or join a club or organization: Volunteering or joining a club or organization can help you meet new people and form new social connections. It's a great way to find people who share similar interests and passions.

3. Take the time to connect with others: In today's fast-paced world, it's important to make time to connect with others. This can be as simple as setting aside time to have a meal with a friend or spending an evening playing a board game with family members.

4. Seek out social support when needed: It's okay to ask for help when you need it. If you're feeling overwhelmed or stressed, reach out to friends or family members for support. They can provide a listening ear, offer practical assistance, or just be there for you when you need it.

5. Practice self-care: Self-care is important for maintaining emotional well-being. Make sure to take time for yourself to do activities that make you feel good, such as reading a book, taking a walk, or listening to music.

6. Spend time in nature: Spending time outdoors in nature can help reduce stress and anxiety and improve mood. Take a break from the hustle and bustle of everyday life and enjoy the beauty of the world around you.

7. Get involved in your community: Participating in activities in your community can help you meet new people and form new connections. This could be anything from attending a local event to volunteering at a community center.

8. Practice kindness and compassion: Showing kindness and compassion to others can help create positive social connections and foster emotional well-being. It could be as simple as holding the door open for a stranger or offering a compliment to someone you know.

9. Reach out to those in need: Volunteering your time to help those in need is a great way to form new social connections and give back to your community. You can also find volunteer opportunities in your area to help out those who are less fortunate.

10. Connect with your spirituality: Taking time to connect with your spiritual beliefs can be a great source of comfort and provide a sense of connection. This could be through attending religious services, meditating, or engaging in other spiritual practices.

Strategies for seeking and finding emotional support supported

Here are some strategies for seeking and finding emotional support:

1. Reach out to loved ones: Often, the people closest to us are the most willing and able to offer emotional support. This might include family members, close friends, or romantic partners. Consider reaching out to these individuals and letting them know how you are feeling. It's okay to be vulnerable and ask for help when you need it.

2. Seek out professional help: If you are struggling with a mental health issue or a difficult life situation, it may be helpful to speak with a therapist or counselor. These professionals are trained to listen and provide support, as well as help you work through your emotions and find healthy ways to cope. Many insurance plans cover therapy, and there are also low-cost or sliding scale options available.

3. Join a support group: Support groups can be a great way to connect with others who are going through similar experiences. These groups provide a safe and non-judgmental space to share your thoughts and feelings and to receive support and encouragement from others. Support groups can be found for a wide range of issues, including mental health conditions, chronic illness, and life transitions.

4. Find online communities: There are many online communities and forums where people can connect with others who are dealing with similar challenges. These communities can be a great source of emotional support, as well as a way to find information and resources. Just be sure to protect your privacy and be cautious about sharing personal information online.

5. Practice self-care: Taking care of yourself is an important aspect of finding emotional support. This might include activities like exercise, healthy eating, getting enough sleep, and finding time to relax and do things you enjoy. These activities can help reduce stress and improve your overall well-being, making it easier to cope with difficult emotions.

6. Seek out community resources: Many communities have resources available for those in need of emotional support. This might include crisis hotlines, support groups, or community centers. These resources can provide a safe and supportive environment, as well as connect you with other individuals and organizations that can help.

7. **Find ways to give back:** Helping others can be a great way to find emotional support, as it can give you a sense of purpose and connection. Consider volunteering your time or resources to a cause you care about, or simply reaching out to a friend or family member in need.

8. **Spend time in nature:** Spending time in nature can be a great way to reduce stress and connect with your emotions. Take a walk in the park, sit and watch the clouds, or just take a few moments to appreciate the beauty of nature. This can be a great way to find emotional support and peace.

9. **Reach out to your faith community:** If you have a religious or spiritual belief system, consider reaching out to your faith community for emotional support. Talking to a leader or a fellow believer can help you find comfort and peace, as well as offer guidance and advice.

10. **Use relaxation techniques:** Relaxation techniques, such as meditation and deep breathing, can help reduce stress and create a sense of inner peace. Consider taking a few moments each day to practice one of these techniques and find emotional support.

11. Journal your thoughts and feelings: Writing down your thoughts and feelings can be a great way to express your emotions and find emotional support. This can be a great tool for self-reflection and can help you gain clarity and insight into your situation.

12. Find a creative outlet: Art, music, and other creative pursuits can be a great way to express your emotions and find emotional support. Consider taking up a new hobby or activity, or just find a few minutes each day to be creative.

13. Talk to a pet: Animals are great listeners, and spending time with your pet can be a great source of emotional support. Cuddling with a furry friend can help reduce stress and provide a sense of comfort and connection.

14. Connect with your inner self: Taking time to connect with your inner self can be a great way to find emotional support. Consider activities like yoga, mindfulness, and meditation, which can help you reconnect with your thoughts and feelings and find peace.

15. Take a break: Taking a break from your daily routine can be a great way to find emotional support. Consider taking a day trip or a weekend getaway, or simply spending an afternoon alone in a quiet place. This can be a great way to give yourself the time and space to focus on your emotions and find clarity.

The role of therapy in exploring and improving emotional well-being

The role of therapy in exploring and improving emotional well-being is significant and multifaceted. Therapy, also known as psychotherapy or counseling, is a process in which an individual engages in regular sessions with a mental health professional to explore and address their emotions, thoughts, and behaviors. The primary goal of therapy is to improve an individual's overall emotional well-being and functioning in their daily life.

Therapy can take many forms, including individual therapy, group therapy, family therapy, and couples therapy. It can be conducted in person, online, or over the phone, and can be provided by a variety of mental health professionals, such as psychiatrists, psychologists, social workers, and licensed mental health counselors.

There are many different approaches to therapy, each with its unique focus and techniques. Some common approaches include cognitive-behavioral therapy (CBT), which focuses on changing negative thought patterns and behaviors; interpersonal therapy (IPT), which focuses on improving communication and relationships with others; and psychodynamic therapy, which focuses on exploring the unconscious mind and early life experiences.

Regardless of the specific approach or setting, therapy involves a collaborative relationship between the individual and their therapist. The therapist serves as a guide and support system, helping the individual to identify and understand their emotions, thoughts, and behaviors and to develop skills and strategies for coping with and improving their emotional well-being.

One of the primary benefits of therapy is that it provides a safe and supportive space for individuals to explore and express their emotions. Emotions can be complex and difficult to understand, and many people struggle to identify and communicate their feelings. Therapy provides a safe and judgment-free environment for individuals to share their emotions and receive feedback and guidance from their therapist.

Therapy can also help individuals to identify and address negative thought patterns and behaviors that may be contributing to their emotional distress. For example, an individual may engage in negative self-talk or engage in unhealthy coping mechanisms, such as substance abuse, to manage their emotions. A therapist can help the individual to recognize and change these patterns and behaviors and to develop more effective coping strategies.

In addition to addressing negative patterns and behaviors, therapy can also help individuals to develop skills and strategies for managing their emotions and improving their overall emotional well-being. These may include relaxation techniques, such as deep breathing and progressive muscle relaxation, or strategies for managing stress, such as time management and problem-solving skills.

Therapy can also be an important resource for individuals who are struggling with specific mental health conditions, such as depression, anxiety, or trauma. These conditions can significantly impact an individual's emotional well-being, and therapy can be an effective treatment option for addressing and managing these issues.

Therapy can be especially beneficial for individuals who are experiencing a challenging life event, such as a loss, a major change, or a relationship issue. These events can be emotionally overwhelming, and therapy can provide a supportive and understanding space for individuals to process and cope with their emotions.

It is important to note that therapy is not a quick fix and may require time and effort to see progress. It is also not right for everyone, and individuals need to find a therapist who is a good fit for them and their needs. Some individuals may also find that therapy is more effective when combined with other treatments, such as medication or self-care practices.

However, therapy plays a crucial role in exploring and improving emotional well-being. It provides a safe and supportive space for individuals to identify and address negative patterns and behaviors and to develop skills and strategies for managing their emotions. Therapy can be an effective treatment option for addressing specific mental health conditions and can be particularly helpful for individuals who are experiencing a challenging life event. While therapy is not a quick fix and may require time and effort to see progress, it can be a powerful tool for improving emotional well-being.

CHAPTER VII.

Conclusion

In conclusion, exploring the depths of emotional well-being is a journey that requires us to delve deep into our inner selves and confront some of the most challenging aspects of our emotions. It is a journey that requires patience, self-compassion, and a willingness to face and work through our emotions. But it is also a journey that can bring us great rewards, as we learn to understand and manage our emotions in healthy ways and develop a greater sense of peace and contentment in our lives.

As we embark on this journey, there are several key things to keep in mind. First and foremost, it is important to remember that we are not alone. There are many resources available to help us along the way, including therapy, self-help books, and support groups. It is also important to seek out the guidance and support of trusted friends and loved ones, who can provide us with the encouragement and perspective we need to keep going.

Another important aspect of this journey is the importance of self-compassion. Too often, we are our own worst critics, beating ourselves up for our perceived shortcomings or failures. But self-compassion involves treating ourselves with kindness and understanding, and recognizing that we are all human and prone to mistakes. By practicing self-compassion, we can learn to be more forgiving of ourselves, and ultimately find greater peace and contentment in our lives.

In addition to self-compassion, it is also important to practice mindfulness. This involves bringing our full attention to the present moment and learning to accept our thoughts and feelings without judgment. By practicing mindfulness, we can learn to be more present in our lives, and find greater peace and happiness as a result.

Finally, it is important to remember that the journey of exploring our emotional well-being requires ongoing effort and commitment. It is not something that can be achieved overnight, but rather something that requires ongoing work and practice. This may involve learning new coping strategies, seeking support when we need it, and finding healthy ways to express and process our emotions. But with persistence and determination, we can learn to navigate the ups and downs of life with greater ease and find greater happiness and fulfillment in the process.

So as you embark on your journey of exploring the depths of emotional well-being, remember to be patient with yourself, seek out the support of trusted friends and loved ones, and practice self-compassion and mindfulness. With time and effort, you can learn to understand and manage your emotions in healthy ways and find greater peace and contentment in your life.

www.ingramcontent.com/pod-product-compliance
Lightning Source LLC
LaVergne TN
LVHW012114160826
845678LV00014B/3093

* 9 7 9 8 3 7 1 4 4 8 8 3 5 *